ODES FOR GRAND PARENTS

ODES FOR GRANDPARENTS

First published in 2012
This edition copyright © Clive Whichelow, 2016

Illustrations by Naomi Tipping

All rights reserved.

Clive Whichelow has asserted his right to be identified as the author of this work in accordance with sections 77 and 78 of the Copyright, Designs and Patents Act 1988.

Summersdale Publishers Ltd
46 West Street
Chichester
West Sussex
PO19 1RP
UK

www.summersdale.com

Printed and bound in China

ISBN: 978-1-84953-848-0

Substantial discounts on bulk quantities of Summersdale books are available to corporations, professional associations and other organisations. For details contact Nicky Douglas by telephone: +44 (0) 1243 756902, fax: +44 (0) 1243 786300 or email: nicky@summersdale.com.

ODES FOR GRAND PARENTS

CLIVE WHICHELOW

ILLUSTRATED BY NAOMI TIPPING

summersdale

CONTENTS

INTRODUCTION

The reason it's called 'grandparenting' is because it's like parenting, only better.

Just think about it: one day these lovely little babies appear, and you haven't had to go through nine months of pregnancy, sleepless nights, staying off alcohol, giving birth and all the rest of it.

When they come to visit it's not you who has to change their nappies, it's Mum and Dad. After a long day playing with them as toddlers, if they start to get a bit fractious you simply say, 'Oh, they're getting a bit tired', and it's Mum and Dad who have to scoop them up and drive home, accompanied by loud bawling and possibly another nappy change on the way.

Your memory of the day will be of playing snap or hide-and-seek and having the excuse to scoff lots of Jammy Dodgers, chocolate fingers and all those other things that grown-ups aren't supposed to eat. You may have enjoyed a fabulous double-bill of Wallace and Gromit and Postman Pat or perhaps something more exotic – who could resist this as a plot summary: 'Igglepiggle and Upsy Daisy join the Tombliboos for a ride on the Pinky Ponk.' Fabulous.

And when they're teenagers and speaking to their parents in a hybrid language of monosyllables and grunts and having hissy fits, they will be unfailingly polite and communicative to you. Why? Well, it's like an unwritten rule, innit?

Oh yes, in being a grandparent you have the best of all possible worlds: you're an honorary kid, while still somehow retaining a modicum of authority. Suddenly all those years of being a parent have finally paid off!

THE 'OLDEN' DAYS

The grandchildren ask about the 'olden days',
When Granny and Grandad were tots.
Do you remember dinosaurs?
Had they invented cots?

Did you wear a gas mask
On your way to school?
Did you own a mobile phone
And were bell-bottoms really cool?

Were you around when Henry the Eighth
Chopped off the heads of his wives?
And you didn't eat pizza or burgers –
What terrible, terrible lives!

Tell us what you remember,
Through your old mind's misty haze.
Tell us again, tell us again,
About the 'olden' days!

GRANNY'S LEARNED TO TXT!

Granny's learned to TXT!
Well! Whatever next?
Concentrating oh-so-hard
And steaming up her specs.

It's fab that Granny's up to date,
She really does us proud.
Though sometimes her best efforts
Make us LOL.

We tell her not to punctuate,
It's just not done you see.
And the use of the semi-colon
Is frankly OTT.

But her skinny granny fingers
Are just the perfect size,
For punching those tiny buttons
That make her strain her eyes.

So when all is said and done
She's an oldie superstar,
And she's now much more than a granny
She's a GR8 grandma!

ISN'T LIFE GRAND?

I swing on the swings when nobody's looking,
I swig on the sherry whenever I'm cooking.
I pull faces at wardens who ticket my car,
I'm politically incorrect while I prop up the bar.

When the grandchildren visit
I'm up to high jinks,
I thrash them at Jenga and tiddlywinks.
I pull away chairs when people sit down,
On Saturday nights I'm painting the town.

The hoodies round here all keep well away,
Their mums tell them I'll lead them astray.
These days I don't bother
to do anything tastefully,
If I've got to grow old I'll do it disgracefully.

HANG-GLIDING GRANDAD

There once was a grandad from Wales,
Who went hang-gliding up in the Dales,
Bird shooters with guns
Thought they'd bagged a big one;
They took the wind right out of his sails.

SPARES

We can't visit our grandparents
Every single weekend,
Mum and Dad say we couldn't,
They'd go round the bend.
Not visiting our grandparents?
It really isn't fair.
But luckily for us you see
We've got another pair.

GRANDCHILDREN

One of 'em's writing on the walls,
Another's throwing up in my slippers;
A third one's juggling my meatballs
And playing football with my kippers.

You love 'em to bits but
they drive you nuts –
Grandchildren can be a pain.
But at the end of the day, no 'ifs', no 'buts',
You can send them home again.

GRANNY
KNOWS BEST

Granny knows best;
Granny knows best;
Eating your greens
Puts hairs on your chest.

Not wearing a woolly
Will give you the flu,
And never wear green
When you're wearing blue.

When making the tea
Always warm the pot,
And never put baby
Face down in the cot.

Eyes close together
Means someone's bad,
And don't I know it –
Look at Grandad!

Never take sweets
From any strange bloke,
And your growth gets stunted
If you smoke.

So teach your kids
When they fly the nest,
You don't need Wikipedia:
Granny knows best.

UNPAID

I was an unpaid skivvy
When my kids were young.
They took it all for granted,
My praises were unsung.

Cooking, washing, ironing –
Picking up from Cubs.
Then, when they reached their teenage years,
Picking up from pubs.

Then all went quiet when they left home,
So why am I so bitter?
Cos now my starring role in life
Is as an unpaid babysitter!

DROPPING OFF

Baby's yawning widely,
Grandma's yawning too;
They've had a long hard morning
And now it's half past two.

They've been playing with the dollies
And eating endless snacks.
It must all get so tiring
And now they need their naps.

The baby or her grandmama?
I don't know who's the worst.
It's a toss-up at this time of day,
Which one will drop off first.

GRANNY AND GRANDAD SONGS

Grandmas and grandads
Used to have songs
On *Top of the Pops*
That made them belong.

St Winnie's school choir
And grandad Clive Dunn
Made my gran and grandad
Think ageing was fun.

Being old and doddery
Is the last straw –
Thank goodness they don't have
Those songs any more.

THE BANK OF GRANDMA AND GRANDAD

Ten quid for their birthdays,
Ten for Christmas Day;
Another ten for Easter,
We're giving it all away!

We love our little grandchildren,
And think we should reward them.
But don't have any more for goodness' sake,
We really can't afford them!

SECOND TIME AROUND

Grannies are much better
Than dads and mums;
They don't make you eat greens
Or finish your sums.

They let you watch telly
And stay up quite late;
Eat sweets by the ton
And drink pop by the crate.

Let you watch films
With zombies and things;
Let you eat ice cream
While swinging on swings.

They weren't easy-going
With your dad or your mum;
But now they're much older
They just want to have fun!

TWENTY-FIRST-CENTURY GRANDAD

Grandads should have beards of white,
Not wear jeans that are too tight.
They should drive three-wheeler cars,
Not souped-up vintage Jaguars.

They should be tucked up by half past nine,
Not up till two, drinking wine.
They should enjoy a gentle croon,
Not the madcap drumming of Keith Moon.

They shouldn't 'get' the modern age,
Nor have their own Facebook page.
They shouldn't Twitter, blog, and such;
A techie grandad's a touch too much!

No, grandads aren't what they used to be,
Don't sit at home drinking tea.
No wonder youngsters get the hump
When Grandad does a bungee jump.

But don't tell Grandad what to do,
'Cos there'll come a day when
you'll be one too.

GRANNY RAP

Well listen up all you kids out there,
I may have wrinkles and a bit of grey hair,
But you mess with me at your peril –
I'm known round these parts as
'No-nonsense Beryl'.

Knock on my door in the
middle of the night,
I'll appear in my curlers – not a pretty sight.
Call me any sort of name
And I'll whack you with my walking frame.

You can throw at me everything you've got,
But it'll be no match for a chamber pot.
My policy is 'shoot to kill',
If the pot doesn't get you the contents will.

I boxed for the county, I think
I've sparred enough,
So come on down if you think
you're hard enough.
If you start swearing I'll tell you to can it,
Didn't you know Granny's
short for 'granite'?

Try what you like, I don't care,
I know you're as yellow as your underwear.
So that's the end of my granny rap,
But don't fanny round
with granny or you'll get a slap!

LITTLE GREY LIES

Grandad's not really asleep,
He says he's resting his eyes.
Do you think we should believe him
Or is it one of his lies?

He's quite an expert fibber,
He lies about his age.
If you say he's past his sell-by date
He gets in quite a rage.

He says he was born after the war,
I don't believe him, do you?
Unless the one he's talking about
Is the Battle of Waterloo.

We all tell white lies once in a while,
So is it such a surprise,
That when you get to Grandad's age
You start on those little grey lies?

DIFFERENT

Old briar pipe and walking stick,
Trousers, boots and vest.
No wonder my friends take the mick –
My gran's different from the rest.

ROD THE MOD'S
A GRANDAD!

Rod the mod's a grandad!
It said so on the news.
Maggie May was shaken
And the jukebox blew a fuse.

Do you think I'm sexy?
He used to ask the fans,
Now he has to ask it
Of their poor old grans.

GRANDAD'S LULLABY

Rock-a-bye Grandad
On the treetop,
If you don't come down soon
We must call the cops.

How you got up there
Nobody knows,
Nothing to do
With the booze, we suppose?

STUFF

Grandmas and grandads have lots of stuff,
It seems they never have enough:

Mantlepiece covered with figurines,
Jubilee mugs of kings and queens,

Old biscuit tins with Constable pics,
Little bowls full of potpourri mix.

Cake stands and doilies, a dish
for the butter,
Newspaper cuttings, all sorts of clutter.

Even the cat has a knick-knack or two:
A mechanical mouse and a toy kangaroo.

Every little thing a cat could boast,
A nice comfy rug and a scratching post.

There's pictures of grandchildren
up by the clock,
A souvenir sporran and a piece of
Brighton rock.

An old china model of Noggin the Nog,
A doorstop that looks like a sausage dog.

Novelty magnets festooned on the fridge,
A postcard showing Sydney Harbour Bridge.

This whole heap of stuff gives
them such pleasure,
We call it rubbish, but they call it treasure.

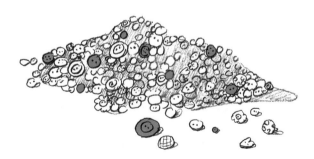

WHEN THEY WERE YOUNG

It's hard to think of Grandad
  Rocking round the clock,
The sight of him in drainpipes
Would give some folk a shock.

It's hard to think of Grandma
  In kaftan, beads and bells,
  Reeking of patchouli oil
  And other exotic smells.

Yes, they were young and foolish once
At the cutting edge of fashion,
Embarrassing their parents,
While in the throes of passion.

But they're much older and wiser now
And tut at our excesses;
It seems to have slipped Grandma's mind
She once wore topless dresses.

And Grandad can't admit
His hair was once so long,
And he used to mooch around the house
Dressed in a sarong.

What else the pair got up to
Heaven only knows, Perhaps
that's why, conveniently,
They find their memory goes.

GRANNY GAMES

My granny's great at games –
Monopoly, Risk and Cluedo.
She's dastardly at draughts,
And she's got a black belt in ludo.

She's sharp at snakes and ladders,
Happy families, rummy and snap.
She's the queen of all the games we play,
From chess to Booby-Trap.

But there's just one game
where she can't match
Me or my little sister,
Come on Gran, face up to it,
You're absolute rubbish at Twister!

THE GRANDCHILDREN ARE COMING!

Lock up the china!
Hide the cat!
Pop in your earplugs!
Clear the knick-knacks!

Keep the mop handy,
Get out the plasters.
Be ready and waiting
For unseen disasters!

Air freshener ready!
Hide the matches!
The grandchildren are coming
Batten down the hatches!

GRAMPZZZ...

Grandad's gone to sleep again,
He's catching forty winks.
He's got to where he doesn't care
What other people think.

He's the king of the sneaky snooze,
A master of deception.
He even slept while standing up
At a dull wedding reception.

You can sit and talk to him
And wait for a reply,
Then give up when you notice
A faraway look in his eye.

He's drifting off to dreamland,
Where grandads rule, OK?
He's like a god in the land of Nod
And everything goes his way.

Barking dogs or road drills,
All the noise you can make;
Once his sights are set on sleep
Nothing'll keep him awake.

He doesn't need a sleeping pill
To get him fast asleep,
And he never has to bother
Counting leaping sheep.

The only exception to this rule
Is after his bedtime drink;
Once he's got his jim-jams on
He can't sleep a bloomin' wink.

GRAND

Our babies are having babies,
Well don't it make you feel old?
I don't mind 'mature'
But I tell you for sure
Not when 'mature' implies mould.

There's a very fine line to be
drawn, it would seem,
'tween 'mature' and 'over the hill'.
Being done up to the nines
And hiding your lines
Is the grandparents' ultimate skill.

Yes, our babies are having babies,
There's a line drawn in the sand.
We can't claim to be
Still young you see
But at last we can say we're grand.

A GRANDPARENT'S LAMENT

I'm sure the years used to be longer,
They come and they're gone in a jiffy.
I may be in *Saga*, but I'm not going gaga,
And my memory's not getting iffy.

The summers are getting much colder,
We used to stay out and play.
I'm older and greyer, but that ozone layer
Wasn't around in my day.

And they say that my taste buds are going,
Just cos I'm long in the tooth.
The bread tastes like hardboard and
cornflakes like cardboard,
Not my imagination – the truth!

Yes, it's all so hard to keep up with,
Things seem to change constantly.
I'm not to blame, I've stayed the same,
Why can't everything be like me?

SLOW

Why are grannies so slow?
Should you wind them up to make them go?
They move round the room
With a great lack of zoom,
How they ever start I don't know.

A GOOD EXAMPLE

Now that I'm a grandma
There are things that I must do:
Not be seen in low-cut tops,
Must cover my tattoo.

I'll have to watch my swearing
And cut down on the fags.
Hide the stubs and cut out pubs,
And stop betting on the nags.

Now that I'm a grandma
I must be whiter than white.
I must set a good example,
Not party night after night.

KINDRED SPIRITS

Grandma and Grandad are just like me,
They don't go to work, they watch TV;
Do jigsaw puzzles and play tiddlywinks,
Even like to have milky bedtime drinks.

They eat lots of sweets and biscuits too,
On long car journeys always need the loo.
Yes, Grandma and Grandad are just like us –
And they even travel free when
they get the bus.

SNAP, CRACKLE AND POP

Grandad always starts the day
With a snap, crackle and pop,
But it's not his breakfast cereal
It's him creaking round the shops!

SUCKING EGGS

Don't teach your granny to suck eggs,
Or so they used to say.
But you know one day you may have to,
If her teeth have gone astray.

PLAYING TRICKS ON GRANDMA

Buttonholes with water squirts,
Whoopee cushions on the chairs;
Scary ghosts in old bedsheets
And skates left on the stairs.

Prank phone calls at dead of night,
He causes such a hoo-ha;
I thought you grandchildren
were bad enough
But Grandad's worse than you are!

MAYHEM

Everything in Grandma's house
Is always trim and neat,
She's even got a fancy cover
For the toilet seat.

She's got different lots of curtains,
Normal ones and nets.
A dropped stitch when she is knitting
Is as untidy as she gets.

But it's quite a different story,
When we grandchildren come to stay.
Granny's good housekeeping
All gets blown away.

Mud over the carpet,
Discarded teddy bears;
Grandad nearly breaks his neck
With the marbles on the stairs.

Squashed Smarties all left on the floor,
Pen marks on the walls;
The overflowing bath looks like
A bubbly Niagara Falls.

No, there's little peace for grandparents
When we grandkids come to stay;
But surely Gran and Grandad
Wouldn't want it any other way?

FOOTBALLING GRANDAD

Grandad's playing football,
Thinks he's Roy of the Rovers.
But Grandad's much too old for this
Look – he's fallen over!

There must be a good reason
Why footballers don't get old.
You don't see grandad transfers,
Where they're bought and sold.

No, when the scouts are scouting
Grandad's no great catch;
And it's such a crime when the injury time
Is longer than the match.

A SEASONAL TIPPLE

Grandad likes his whisky,
Grandma likes her gin;
Just at Christmas
That is, of course,
Then it's not a cardinal sin.

But does Christmas start in August,
April, March or May?
Like Roy Wood
They wish it could
Be Christmas every day!

GRANNY'S GARDENING

Grandma likes her garden,
She spends hours and hours
Up to her knees in pulled-out weeds
In sunshine and in showers.

She deadheads all the roses,
No mercy does she show,
And if she's feeling generous
She lets me have a go.

Spraying all the bugs and pests,
No one will escape.
The garden should be cordoned off
With the coppers' crime-scene tape.

Thrashing, chopping, burning –
Grandma doesn't care.
All the cats in the neighbourhood
Stay away when she's out there.

After that she has a snooze,
Says we'll play some games a bit later.
Indoors she's just a pussycat
But out there: The Terminator!

GRANDMA'S FOR TEA

We're going off to Grandma's,
We're going there for tea.
They haven't changed the tablecloth
Since 1953.

They have doilies on the tables,
Cushions on the chairs;
A mangle in the garden
And stair rods on the stairs.

The toilet's got a cover,
The sink has old face flannels.
You can't plug in the kettle
And the TV's just five channels.

But when it comes to teatime,
I hope that on my plate,
The food's the only thing in the house
Not past its sell-by date!

WILDLIFE

The grandparent is a strange old beast,
It feeds on tea and cake;
It rattles round the house at night
And sleeps when it should be awake.

Its habitat is a sofa,
And it often hunts in pairs;
Seeking out the half-price deals
Amongst the high street's wares.

It's time Sir David Attenborough
Made a documentary,
About the life of the aged grandparent,
On the BBC.

You can keep your pandas,
Your lions and giraffes –
The life of the aged grandparent
Would give us all a laugh.

GRANDCHILDREN'S DUTIES

Grandmas get muddled,
Sometimes they're befuddled,
It's due to their age, they say.
But that's all right,
Just hold them tight,
They're there to be cuddled, OK?

WHAT DO THEY DO WHEN WE'RE NOT THERE?

Grandma and Grandad sit in a chair,
But what do they do when we're not there?

Do they roll back the carpet
and dance till dawn
Or get drunk and wake up parked
out on the lawn?

Do they play poker for very high stakes
Or go jet-skiing over vast lakes?

Do they hang round the dodgier pubs
Or get thrown out of swanky nightclubs?

Do they pose naked for the local art school
Or sit in a chair and do nothing at all?

PHOTOS

Grandad shows us photos
Of him so long ago,
When he was young and had dark hair
Before his ears began to grow.

Grandma too was young once
Before she had her specs,
Both so slim and stylish
They looked like Posh and Becks.

But just one thing still puzzles me
It doesn't seem quite right,
When exactly did they change
To colour from black and white?

GRAB A GRANNY

When Granny got drunk
She grabbed hold of some hunk
And made him dance the lambada.
Then the Charleston, the twist,
How could he resist?
Then they tried something harder.

They did the bolero,
The rumba, the tango,
The crowd all shouted for more.
Then like some young bimbo
She tried to limbo
Under the toilet door.

Oh what a disgrace,
There's a time and a place
For showing you're hale and hearty.
It's not playing ball
To embarrass us all
At your granddaughter's birthday party.

SEEING

Grandma's so short-sighted,
She's as blind as a bat.
She wipes her feet on her pet dog
And says 'hello' to the mat.

She pours salt into her coffee
And sugar on her chips,
She used a Magic Marker
To brighten up her lips.

When you tell her she's short-sighted
She says, 'Really? Oh, I see.'
But don't talk nonsense Grandma –
You don't see, don't you see?

GRANDCHILDREN'S PAINTING

Oh no! The grandchildren want to paint!
They say they're careful,
but I know they ain't.
With a splish and a splosh and
a splonk and a splat,
Last time we ended up with a Day-glo cat.

Jackson Pollock's got nothing on them,
His action paintings look like gems
Of order, restraint, and *je ne sais quoi*,
Not World War Three straight out of a jar.

The lampshade's now pink
with purple specks,
The budgies have blue, black
and bright-red necks.
The grandchildren painting look so angelic,
While the whole front room
has turned psychedelic.

The entire place is in a terrible state,
But to them it's like their
own wing of the Tate.
It's hard to say 'no' when
they want to paint,
But to put up with this you must be a saint.

YOUNG GRANDAD

It takes some getting used to,
Being called 'Grandad'.
I've only just got used to
Being called simply 'Dad'.

I just don't feel I'm old enough
To be called 'grand' anything;
I've still got all my hair and teeth
And wear baseball caps and bling.

I can show those kids a thing or two
   On skateboards or computers;
I'll even teach them how to do
   Wheelies on their scooters.

If you must call me 'Grandad'
   Please do it quietly;
I really don't feel old enough:
   I'm only sixty-three.

THE KNOWLEDGE

Grandad's good with wood,
All sorts of DIY;
He knows the names of flowers
And the birds as they fly by.

He can reel off all the dates
Of battles, kings and queens;
He knows how to fix a leaky tap
And grow rows of runner beans.

He knows almost everything,
Even knows about the unknown;
So how come he knows less than me
About his mobile phone?

HAVING GRANDCHILDREN

Did you hear that our
Deirdre's got pregnant again?
That's fourteen, and counting,
she thinks it's a pain.

She moans of the things
that it will be affecting,
You can't drink so much
wine when you're expecting.

She says that last time she
was practically raving,
Eating the coal to satisfy cravings.

She got tired out walking up stairs,
And had to stock up on more teddy bears.

Nappies and dummies and new Babygros,
Curling up in the daytime
and having a doze.

Just having a baby, oh what a fuss!
We've had lots of grandchildren
– it ain't bothered us!

WAKE-UP CALL

You still wear tight jeans
And know how to have fun,
And you're still listening
To Radio 1,
You'll be out on the town
Whenever you can,
But you remember you're old
When they call you 'Gran'!

BUTTON BOX

Grandma's got a button box,
It makes a lovely noise;
You shake it up and tip them out,
It's better than all my toys.

Black and brown and purple,
Red and green and blue;
Yellow, mauve and aubergine,
Buttons of every hue.

There's silver ones and gold ones,
Some are made with cloth;
Some are old and some are new,
Some nibbled by the moths.

It's like a box of treasure,
From some old pirate ship;
I think I'll put a button box
On my Christmas list.

GRAND WISDOM

We're old and wise and venerable,
So when the grandchildren come to call,
We have years of knowledge to dispense,
Not to mention common sense.

So come, grandchildren, ask away,
We can keep this up all day,
We're as knowledgeable as can be,
Unless it's new technology.

DOWNSIZING

Granny always said she'd like to
Downsize if she could,
Rattling round a great big house
Was doing her no good.

Well she's still there in the same old house,
But she's downsized now, for sure:
She used to be but five foot three
And now she's four foot four!

SLEEPOVER AT GRANNY'S

They look so sweet and innocent,
  Curled up in their beds;
  In their best pyjamas,
  Cuddling their teds.

Who'd have thought an hour ago
  They'd given me the vapours;
  Nearly burnt the house down
  And made the morning papers?

Screaming, raving, ranting
Like an inner-city riot;
But some brandy in their bottles
Seemed to get them quiet.

Let's all hope at last now
They'll sleep, perchance to dream;
Cos I swear that if they wake up again
It'll be Granny's turn to scream.

GRANDAD'S STORIES

Grandad's got some stories,
Oh, the stories he can tell,
About the amazing life of Grandad
He swears they're true, as well.

His trip along the Amazon,
His climb of Everest;
All the medals he can't quite find
Once displayed upon his chest.

His run-in with a hungry lion,
Being star of stage and screen;
His time as a child prodigy
And all the stuff in between.

Grandad's got more stories
Than a giant office block;
And if you sneer at what you hear
He's got plenty more in stock.

NOISE

Mum says I'm much too noisy,
Dad says I'm way too loud,
But Gran doesn't mind the volume,
She just turns her hearing aid down.

TEENAGE GRANDCHILDREN

They've got plugs in their ears
And mobile phones,
Electronic games
They play on their own.

All you get from them's
An occasional bleep,
They talk more than this
When they're fast asleep!

The art of conversing
Got lost one fine day,
But as soon as they're hungry
They'll find something to say!

SECOND CHILDHOOD

Grandad's doing a jigsaw,
Grandma's playing with dolls,
Then we'll have a tea party
With pop and sausage rolls.

Then we'll all play hide-and-seek
And murder in the dark,
Then we'll play at dressing up
Or feed ducks in the park.

Some say getting older
Is really quite a pain,
But once you're a gran and a grandad
You just get young again.

GRANNY'S MUSIC COLLECTION

Gran's got these things called 'records',
They're big and round and black;
She's got hundreds and
hundreds and hundreds,
Stored on her 'record rack'.

They all look quite impressive,
Lined up in their rows;
But how she fitted them in her iPod
We shall never know.

TREASURE ISLAND

The sofa's now a pirate ship,
With old bedsheets as sails;
The Jolly Roger flying
In the storms and gales.

The garden's Treasure Island,
Where lies the treasure pot;
Let's hope they don't find the shovel
And dig up the flipping lot!

GRANDMA'S RULES

Elbows off the table,
Make sure you sit up straight;
Don't you speak till you're spoken to,
Eat everything on your plate.

Leave greens and there's no pudding,
Don't say 'can', say 'may';
Yes, Grandad has to watch his step,
'Cos Grandma rules, OK?

SHHH...

Isn't it peaceful? Isn't it quiet?
The grandchildren have gone, just listen...
The silence is eerie,
And though we feel weary,
As soon as they've gone we miss 'em!

ODES FOR
OLDIES

CLIVE WHICHELOW

ODES FOR OLDIES

Clive Whichelow

£7.99

Hardback

ISBN: 978-1-84953-847-3

Whether you're just going grey or growing old disgracefully, this collection of comical verse on all things oldie is the perfect pick-me-up!

If you're interested in finding out more about our books, find us on Facebook at **Summersdale Publishers** and follow us on Twitter at **@Summersdale**.

www.summersdale.com